Twisted Depression

Celeste Ross

I0790451

Introduction

Twisted Depression is a story about two women who live with some form of depression. The struggles they go through and how they deal with them every day. One woman starts questioning life as she enters the "empty nest" phase. The other woman faces tragedy and tries to deal with what happens next. Both women will come face to face with the realities of life. What they choose to do about it, well that is what makes the difference. We all must make choices in life. These choices decide what path of life we will take.

Dedication

To God my Father and creator and to everyone who has inspired me to follow my dreams: my parents Sanders and Janie (2019) Ross, siblings Sanders Jr. (2003) and Rowena, children Sheree and Malik, and spiritual mentor author Minister Stephanie Captain: brillanthumans.org

Table of Contents

Dreams

I didn't care too much about being by myself. I had no choice since my children were all teenagers now. They had interests and friends and sadly I was left out. Gone were the days when they would cling to my side. Crying,

"Mommy don't leave me!"

Now it's more like,

"Bye, Mom, see you tomorrow.

So, it is no wonder that I would get very excited around major holidays: Thanksgiving, Christmas, and Easter. Those are the special times that fill the house with friends and family. I used to include birthdays, but my children now go out with friends. I make sure that I pull out all the tricks when I have company. You find yourself doing this when you are alone most of the time. I guess this is what happens when you allow your children to be independent. I always encouraged them to get out and meet people. Do things that I have never done. Some people criticize me for being this way. My son is 19 and is a college freshman. My daughter is 16 and a sophomore in high school. Why would I want to hold them back?

I grew up not being able to experience true freedom. I couldn't participate in after-school activities because I had to get home. It was hard to keep friends. I had no trouble making friends, but I could not keep them. No one wants a friend who cannot do anything. No school dances, no games, and no dating, and therefore, no friendships were established. I did not make long-lasting friendships until I attended college and started working. No, I did not fault my parents because they did what they did with what they knew.

So, I always decided that when I had children, I would give them the freedom to enjoy life to the fullest. I encouraged them to get out of the house. Going to school was just the beginning: church functions, sports teams, sleepovers, birthday parties, and dating. I wanted my children not to grow up socially awkward. I enjoyed every milestone: first steps, first time riding the school bus, the loss of the first tooth, puberty, first kiss, first heartbreak, first pet, first dance, first time playing a sport, recitals, learning to drive, first trip with a friend, and now I am waiting for them to move out and begin a new chapter in their lives.

I am lonely and depressed at times. That is the price I must pay for my children to be happy. There are perks to doing what I did. I have children who have bonded with others and have meaningful relationships. I have acquired so many other adopted children because their friends call me mom. Their parents respect me. I love it. It may not mean that I have physical beings around me. What it does mean is that I have people to talk to on the phone, on social media, and even in letters. Don't get me wrong, I do go out and have fun. It's just that when the fun is over and I go home if the children are not there, I am alone.

I often dream about being surrounded by friends and family. I wish that my house had a continuous flow of people and actions. I know some would not care for that, but I have had my share of quiet and being by myself. I do my best dreaming in the kitchen. I started daydreaming the other day while washing the dishes.

There I was in the kitchen washing dishes. I always open the curtains to let the sunshine in. I really can't stand my kitchen to be dark. There I stood looking out the window. Our house is kind of secluded. We have neighbors but they are a good 3-to-5-minute walk away. Behind the house is a small set of woods. It is a beautiful home. It is a small 3-bedroom house. I love the coziness of it. Last winter we bought an electric fireplace for the living room. I love to sit there looking at the fire. However, most of my time is spent in my bedroom. I do not have the master room. I gave that room to my daughter. She loves to have friends over, so they all fit nicely in that big room.

Let me tell you more about my house. I have a large country front porch. My son put up a screen, so it is nice at night. It protects me from bugs. I have a swing and a comfortable sofa on the porch. The house did have some faults, but nothing too serious. Many trees surround the house. When I get enough money, I will have some of those large trees cut down. The house only has a couple of windows. I wish it had more than that because I love sunlight. That is another project for another day. The backyard is a little uneven. When we have heavy rain, it makes a puddle near the fence.

I am not complaining but I dream of a big house with a perfectly designed landscape. I want a home with many windows, and doors, a big front and back porch, and a garage because I have a carport. I guess everyone dreams about something. I say that to make myself feel better.

Well, let me tell you a little bit about myself. I am a single mother of two wonderful children Red and Cynthia. Their father died some years ago. I always wished that we would have been married before he left. So, another dream of mine is to have a big wedding. I am currently not working so my life is a little bit boring. I have almost the same routine every day. I wake up, bring my daughter to school (which will change soon because she is learning how to drive), go walking, come home clean and cook, and pick up my daughter, if there are any activities at church then I go to that, come home, watch a little tv or play on my phone, and then it is bedtime. A wonderful life I have. A dear friend of mine encouraged me to write a book. That is what I am trying to do. It's funny I never dreamt of being an author and here I am!

Let me take you back to an incident that happened to me years ago. There I was in the kitchen as usual. I was washing the dishes and staring out of the window. The woods always look so dark and gloomy even in the daytime. I watched the trees sway in the wind. The leaves all moved as if they were dancing. I sometimes stare as if I could see something. Something in the thick of the trees, but there was never anything there.

Then one day I thought I saw something, a black shadow. It seemed to be hiding behind one of the trees. The tree was far away, but I saw something. I had to go investigate. I went outside into the backyard to get a better look. I searched but I saw nothing. The ground was not disturbed. I gave up and went inside. Cynthia was in the kitchen.

"Hey, mom. What are you doing outside?" she said as she was pouring milk into her bowl of cereal.

"I was looking at the ground. I thought I saw something, but I was wrong," I said as I threw my coat on the back of one of the kitchen chairs. "I thought I saw a black shadow behind one of the trees in the wood."

Cynthia went to the window. She leaned over to get a good look.

"Mom, I don't see anything. Maybe it was a bird, or you are daydreaming again," she said as she shrugged her shoulders and walked away.

"Yes, you are right. I probably just thought I saw something. It could be a vulture or a bear," I picked up my coat and hung it in the closet. Then a thought came to my head. A BEAR! I hope not. I am often alone in this house and would be scared to go to my car.

Days went by and I saw nothing. We went out of town for a little break. When we got back home, I noticed that the kitchen curtains were open. I went to close it when I saw the shadow again. There it was near the third tree on the right.

"Cynthia! Come here quickly," I screamed trying not to lose focus on the shadowy figure.

I heard Cynthia running. "Yes, Mom," she said out of breath.

"Look there behind the third tree over there. See the shadow?" I said with excitement. She would finally see that I was not daydreaming.

Cynthia bent forward and squinted her eyes. Shaking her head she said," Sorry Mom I do not see anything. Are you sure it is not a bird? Maybe it flew away by the time I got here."

She stood up and looked at me.

"Maybe you are right. Maybe it was a bird." I closed the curtains and tried not to look disappointed. Just then the phone rang. I picked it up.

"Hello," I said into the phone. Yes, we still have a landline phone. Do not laugh. It was my son Red, on the phone, who was away at college.

"Hey, Mom. It is good to hear from you. I am still coming home next week for a break, but I wanted to know if my roommate could come also. His parents forgot and booked a cruise for that weekend, and he does not feel like being alone. So, I told him to let me see if it was okay. Is it? "

"Yes, he can come. I just need to verify it with his parents. I have no problems with him coming." I said happily. I love having company.

Family

The days were going by so quickly. I was so excited for the company. I was cleaning, decorating, and preparing food. I do that and store it in the freezer to have more time to enjoy my guests. Then around Wednesday, I received a phone call from my cousin in South Carolina. There is a bad storm heading their way and they wanted to know if they could seek refuge at my house. I had to hide my excitement. I immediately agreed and was looking forward to seeing them. I forgot to ask how many would be coming, but it is okay, we will make room.

I soon found out that they expected the storm around Friday evening. So, they were coming on Thursday! There will be eight of them, plus my son and his roommate, and then there will be my daughter and me. Twelve people to entertain. Well, eleven I do not have to count myself. I was especially happy to know that my favorite little cousin Keisha and her three-month-old baby were coming. I love babies. They just bring so much joy into a home.

The weatherman predicted heavy winds and rain for my area. This must be a bad storm if we feel some of the aftermath. I live about 3 hours away from them. I had plenty of water and non-perishable foods, I had plenty of already prepared meals in the freezer, and big containers of dry lemonade mix. I also had board games, card games, and a karaoke machine. Yes, indeed I was ready.

Red arrived first with his roommate Donald. Then a little towards the afternoon, my cousins started pouring in. My cousin Ricky pulled up first with his grill on a hitch on the back of his truck. Ricky and I were the same age and kind of grew up like brother and sister. We have a close relationship. Then his wife Beverly pulled up in the car with their children: Peter and Katelyn.

I watched the cars pull up into the driveway. Ricky stopped his truck and jumped out.

"Hey! Who is watching the store?" Ricky said as he walked towards me.

"You can't leave that junk in my yard. It will cost you one hug and a kiss," I said as I wrapped my arms around his neck and kissed him on the cheek. Then I went to hug Beverly and the children.

"Where are the others?" I asked as we started getting their luggage out of the vehicles.

"They are so slow," Beverly said as she shook her head.

"We all started together, but no, they had to stop at the outlet in the other town." Beverly was at this time leaning against her car. "I tried telling them that there are stores here too."

We all laughed as we walked towards the house with the luggage. Then I turned to Beverly and said,

"Well, it is alright. Because now you guys get the first pick of the bedrooms. They will have the leftovers or the living room."

I directed Beverly to the rooms and allowed her to pick which room they would have. Once we got them all settled into the rooms. We went out to the living room and sat down. Just then Ricky jumped up and slapped Red on the shoulder.

"Hey, come on, let us men go prepare the yard for tonight's cookout. So, get the rake. Do you guys have a leaf blower?" Ricky asked Red as he started to walk out the front door.

"Man, we have everything. It's all in the shed in the backyard. "

Red then looked back at Beverly, Cynthia, Katelyn, and me as we were sitting on the sofa.

"I guess you women can relax. We men are going to take care of dinner tonight. Come on Donald. You are not on vacation dude," Red took little Peter by the hand and led him outside. He opened the door and standing in front of the door about to ring the doorbell was Keisha. I jumped up to go hug her when I was pushed out of the way by Cynthia. She was running to the van to get the baby. I hugged Keisha and walked her into the house. Then I remembered my other cousins were outside. So, Beverly and I went outside to help them.

"Hey, Albert! So, glad you guys made it."

I hugged him and went over to my cousin Eloise and hugged her. Cynthia came over to me with the baby.

"Mom, ain't he so adorable? Look at his beautiful eyes." Cynthia was holding him up to her face.

"Oh, yes, he is so handsome," I said as I reached over and pinched his soft chubby cheeks.

"Cynthia bring him indoors out of this cool air. "I then turned around because I could hear the men fussing about my yard in the background. I just shook my head and went to the van to help get the luggage and stuff out.

"Hey, Albert," Ricky said as he came from the backyard up to the front.

"What in the heck took y'all so long to get here? Probably trying to get out of helping to clean and cook." Ricky hugged Albert as we were all laughing at this time.

"Naw, I wished that was the reason. These women were shopping their butts off. Look at all this junk they got. I think they think we are going to be staying for months instead of days," Albert started to walk Ricky over to the van to see all the bags in the trunk.

The men continued to clean the yard and set the barbeque. The women were in the house putting up groceries and deciding on what sides to make to go with dinner. I did notice that Keisha and Donald now and then gave each other a look of interest. I thought it was cute and just smiled. It was funny I did not see any shadows in the woods that day. Oh, we had a wonderful time. Dinner was amazing! We had ribs, chicken, potato salad, Cole slaw, corn on the cob, and homemade strawberry ice cream. What a feast. We ate, we laughed, we told stories, and we just enjoyed being together. I am so sorry it took a storm to get us together, but I must admit I was so happy.

Once we cleaned up. We put the children to bed. I helped wash and rocked the baby to sleep. Oh, it was so wonderful having a baby and little children in the house again. I miss that special bonding time when Cynthia and Red were small. We all gathered in the living room. However, the older children went to the back room which was set up as a game room.

In the game room, they were playing pool. Red was good at the game and was showing off his move to Donald. Donald did not mind because he loved the attention that Keisha was giving to him. Cynthia broke the spell when she asked,

"Does anybody besides me want anything to drink and a snack?"

"I do want a drink. Well, you can't have the kind of drink that I want. Red do you or Donald want a drink with a little kick to it?" Keisha asked them as she got up from the sofa. Her eyes fixed on Donald.

"Yes," both men said practically at the same time. While Keisha was mixing up drinks Cynthia was gathering herself a drink and snacks. Red and Donald started to talk while they were alone.

"Red, does your cousin have a boyfriend or is still entangled with the baby's father?" Donald said as he reached over to set the pool balls up again.

"No, as far as I know, she is single. Why dude you trying to creep on my cousin?" Red now leaning over the balls getting ready to break.

"Kind of yeah. She is so pretty and easy to talk to. Besides, I see her checking me out." Donald said with a smile while he waited for his turn. Just then the girls arrived back with the drinks and snacks.

"Let me warn you my drinks have a good kick to them. So, if you boys don't think you are man enough to handle them. You better not drink them. "Keisha passed both of them a cup.

"Wait!" screamed Red. "What is Cynthia drinking? It, better not be alcohol or I'll kill her!" He said bending over to smell her cup. He forgot that technically they were all underaged.

"Whatever, I have soda. You're not my father you know. Besides, I am not stupid enough to drink before you." Cynthia said as she grabbed her cup and two cookies and sat back on the sofa.

"Wow! This drink has a kick. Daddy likes." Donald said as he raised his red cup and tapped it against Keisha's red cup. She then turned around and tapped Red and Cynthia's cup. Just then the baby started crying.

"I will check on him," Cynthia said as she jumped up. She placed her cup on the table and ran to the room to get the baby before anyone else. I then came from around the corner. Cynthia pushed me against the wall.

"Get out of my way old lady," Cynthia said laughing as she passed me.

"Girl, you better give me that baby after you change his diaper. I hope he pooped a nice full diaper for you to change." I said as I turned around and went back into the living room.

I sat back down next to Beverly. I had to admit I was very happy to have the house filled with all these people. Hearing the children in the room playing when they were supposed to be sleeping. The young adults laughed in the game room and we adults in the living room singing and dancing to the oldies. This is all that I want. I wish it could last forever. The later it got we started dropping off like flies. I finally settled down to bed around 3 am.

The next morning, I was awakened by the cries of a baby. I missed that sound. Cynthia stayed in the room with me since we had so much company. I tried to slide out of bed so not to wake her up, but I did.

"Good morning, sweetheart, I am sorry to have woken you up," I said to Cynthia. Then I bent over and kissed her on the forehead. I started to walk towards my bathroom when I heard a loud boom! I looked outside and it was pouring down raining, the wind was heavy, and it was dark and gloomy. The storm was here. It was kind of scary. I put on my robe and went out to check on everyone else. When I opened the door, I was hit with the pleasant smell of food cooking.

"Did anyone hear that loud sound? Oh, no there it goes again. Is that thunder?" Keisha was now standing in the hall with a look of concern on her face.

"Yes, it is a storm outside," Ricky said. "I have been following the news all morning. It is really bad back home. However, here is a flood warning. This storm is not playing. "Ricky shook his head and headed towards the kitchen. Just then Beverly came out of the kitchen.

"Hey, sleepy heads. I made breakfast if anyone was hungry. The children and I have been up for hours. They even woke up the baby. So, he is all dressed and fed also," Beverly pointed at the children sitting in front of the television.

I went back to my bedroom to get washed up. Cynthia was now up and combing her hair.

"What is all the noise?" she asked me.

"The loud banging is the storm outside. The loud laughing is the children looking at the television. Did I answer all your questions? Ms. Lady." I put my hand on Cynthia's head and shook it. Then I proceeded to go into the bathroom.

I went into the dining room, and everyone was sitting around the table. They were eating, talking, and laughing. Cynthia, Red, Donald, Keisha, Beverly, and Ricky were all looking at me as I entered the room. I grabbed a plate from the end of the table and started to get my food. I mean Beverly went all out. There were pancakes, sausage patties, scrambled eggs, biscuits, and cheese grits. After we all ate everyone separated into their groups. The small children played on the screened-in back porch for a little while since it was cold outside. The young adults were in the game room and we older adults were in the living room sitting in front of the fireplace.

Conversations were about the same topics we told numerous stories about our lives. Reminiscing about the quirky stuff that our children do. I was amazed and pleased to see that Cynthia helped Keisha with the cleaning of the kitchen. Everything was so calm and peaceful. You might also say it was calm before the storm.

The Storm

Just then we heard a big boom! We went running to the window. My neighbor's trash can was sailing down the street and crashed into another neighbor's mailbox. The impact knocked the mailbox over like it was a feather. Hearing this all the children young and old came running. The baby was with us in the living room, but he started to cry. Red turned on the television to watch the weather channel. We first watched what was happening in my area. Heavy winds and rain. Temperatures in the forties. There was also a tornado and flood warnings for the county next to me. They predicted that this would be an all-day occurrence. Then Red turned to a channel which was following the storm in South Carolina. Storm

Sandy was her name. She was a mad storm wreaking havoc where she landed. Since my cousins live in a tourist area the weather station or storm chasers, I should say, kept giving updates on their area. This was just the first day and the full impact of the storm would not be reached until tomorrow afternoon. Right now, the winds were picking up to about 90 mph. Trees and powerlines in some areas were already down. Heavy rainfalls were causing flooding in many areas in the downtown section of town. The governor was calling for everyone to evacuate. The news was expecting this to be a record-breaking storm. I looked at their faces and could see that they were very concerned and scared. I mean who wouldn't be? Your livelihood was being destroyed and there was nothing that you could do about it. We were fixed on the tv for hours. Watching what was happening here and watching what was going on there. It was a mess in both areas. I was just glad that I did not have to face it alone with just my children. It was nice having men in the house. They went around securing the house. Making sure windows and doors were locked and boarded. The shed was closed. Yesterday they cut down and trimmed the branches on the trees close to the house. Louise, being a nurse was going over some survival suggestions with us. Beverly, Cynthia, Keisha, and I made sure we had food and drinks prepared. We placed candles all over the house in case the lights went out. Everyone charged up their phones, iPads, and laptops, and we put batteries in all flashlights. To get our minds off the storm we started to play games. One of my favorite games to play is something like Password. We pass out pieces of paper and everyone writes down words for us to guess. Then they are folded and placed in a box. The box has a small hole on top. The hole is just big enough to reach your hand in and pull out a paper. Then we break into teams. Each team picks a person who will guess what the word is from the clues given by each team. The team that guesses the most words wins. We played other games like Uno and Monopoly. The hours just flew by. Then around 6 pm, we sat down for dinner. We were doing good. We stopped looking at the weather reports. Instead, we just enjoyed being together. After dinner, we decided to watch TV. Just then we heard the rain starting again. The wind picked up too. The windows would rattle from the weight of the wind blowing against it.

The TV started flickering. We cut it off and just talked some more. Finally, after a day of worrying and playing games, we were tired and started preparing to go to bed. While Keisha took her shower. I washed the baby and prepared him for bed. I loved it. The smell of baby powder and baby lotion fills up the atmosphere. The cueing noises that he made. Then I held him and gave him his bottle. Oh, I truly missed this time with my children. The way babies look at you with so much trust in their eyes. The way they snuggle up under your neck when you hold them. Yes, I was having baby fever. Once I laid him down, I went to get myself ready for bed. I was tired and nervous over the storm.

The next morning, I was awakened by the sound of Eloise's voice screaming.

"Oh! My God!" She was in her bedroom watching TV. I knocked on the door to see what the matter was. The door opened and there was Albert, Ricky, Beverly, and Eloise sitting in the room watching the news. I stuck my head in and asked,

"Is everything okay?" I asked as I looked around at all their faces. I knew everything wasn't okay, but I guess we must ask that question. Eloise looked at me and pointed at the TV. The storm chaser was showing a video of how the storm was ripping through the street. It wasn't just any street. It just happened to be the street where Ricky's Construction business was located. Albert also worked with Ricky and about 50 other employees. He saw a glance at the building as the camera went down the street. The roof was off, and it looked like half of the building was gone. The rest of the street was a disaster. Trees were down. One was in the middle of the street. Another was lying across another business' rooftop. Powerlines were down. A car flipped over, and another was on top of another car. Water was everywhere. Then the news showed another part of town near the beach. It was a ghost town. Most of the people left, but of course, every storm you have the same group that refuses to leave. An elderly couple was trapped inside their house because the door to the bathroom where they were hiding was jammed. The storm was picking up speed. It was incredible. I am not too sure about the technical terms used but I heard F-4 tornado and worst storm since the 1980s. I felt so bad for my cousins. This was their homes, their jobs, their schools, and their lives that we were looking at. I just wanted to cry. I had no words to say. All I could do was cover my mouth. Just then there was a knock at the door. We all got up to go see who it could be in this bad weather.

I looked through the peephole and there was no one there. So, I slowly opened the door. It was hard with the wind fighting against me. Albert and Ricky pushed me aside and they stepped onto the porch. Albert looked around and said,

"Would you just look at this mess?" He was gesturing for all of us to come on the porch.

The rain and wind were splashing up against the house. We were getting wet but we stood there frozen. A big branch from the tree had landed on the porch. The trash can that used to be at the front of the driveway was now near the backyard fence. Trash and leaves were everywhere. I looked down the street and one of my neighbors had a little shed for their children to play in was now in the street flipped upside down. I turned and walked back into the house. When we all got in the house we were just stunned. Just then Beverly started to cry and Eloise sat down beside her. Eloise was rubbing Beverly's back to try to calm her down. The men finally came back in to give us a report.

Ricky said, "It is not too bad. I do not see any damage to the cars or your house. However, a piece of your fence is knocked down. A big tree branch fell across it. That cheap grill that you had on the side of the house. Somehow the top is broken off." Ricky then looked at me and smiled. He then sat down next to his wife.

Beverly stopped crying and looked around at all of us.

"I am sorry. I just got so overwhelmed. I was thinking about the mess outside and then my mind wandered home and the disaster that was waiting for us there. It got the best of me and I just let go. I am better now. I just want to forget about it. Enjoy what I have now and move on. So, please can we forget about the news for the rest of the day? Let us eat and be merry." Beverly tried her best to smile.

I got up from the sofa and walked towards the kitchen.

" Ok, I am going in here and warm up a feast!" I said with a smile on my face.

The rest of the day went well. The lights went out around 8 pm but we just lit the candles and sat in front of the fireplace. We had a night full of jokes, stories, and laughter. Once again I had the pleasure of putting the baby asleep. I placed him in the crib and just looked at that sweet face. I kissed him on the forehead, put my hand on his chest, and did a quick night prayer over him.

The next day we had no lights for almost the entire day. The internet went off for a while but finally came back on around 3 pm. There was still a restriction for them to enter back into their town. So, they decided to stay a couple of more days. The damage from the storm was minor in my area. We all chipped in and cleaned up the yard. Ricky took great pleasure in throwing away my outside grill. He never did like those cheap grills, but hey, that is all that I can afford. We were blessed to still have a great amount of food and water.

The next day was even better. The sun was out. It made the day much warmer than the previous days. The lights were back on and the internet was working well. The yard was clean and all broken tree limbs were picked up. We were using them for fire. Their phones were constantly ringing with news of back home. Albert and Ricky decided that they would leave tomorrow. Ricky needed to get back and assess the damages to his properties to file insurance claims. I was sad to hear this but I knew that I would be making a trip there soon.

I took advantage of having the baby still with me. I barely put him down. Cynthia would compete with me for his affections. We were all sad that the fun was ending but all good things have to come to an end. I was just happy that they all came to stay with me. I have other family there, but they hardly ever come to visit with me.

I helped them pack their belongings into their vehicles. My family always packs the night before leaving. That way we can stay up late and don't have to rush on the day of the trip. We had another great day and night. This time we barbequed on the grill. Everyone including the children stayed up as late as our bodies allowed. This would be a visit that I would never forget.

Once the children were down we adults continued our visit. The young adults went into the game room and we older adults this night sat in the den.

The den was a cozy little room. My husband used to use it as a man cave. Since his passing, I have used it as a writing room. There was a small desk with a computer, a sofa, and an electric fireplace. There was a nice big window facing the backyard where I loved to sit and daydream looking out the window.

There we were sitting wrapped in blankets. I started the conversation by asking, when they arrived home what would they see?

"I expect to see so much damage. One of the guys who works with us called me yesterday and informed me that the roof and part of the building are destroyed. Plus, there is flooding on the street where our house is located. So, I have a lot of work to do. I am so glad that I paid for expensive insurance. To make sure that I am covered," Ricky said as he laid his head in his hands.

Albert sat up straight and began to respond to Ricky.

"Well, you are not alone boss. You know we are here for you. All we can do is take it one day at a time because I do not want you and Beverly overwhelmed. We can replace materials, but we cannot replace people." Albert then reached over and gave Ricky a high five.

"I know that we have a mess when we get home, but we will rejoice in the fact that we have our lives. So many people have died or were injured but we were blessed to have made it through alive and well," Eloise said as she smiled and looked at each of us.

We changed the subject and just started talking about the future. We were planning future gatherings. At the time we were in the den planning a calendar. The young adults were having their fun in the game room. You could hear them laughing and cracking jokes loudly from the game room. I did notice several times that Keisha and Donald went outside to talk. They sure have been getting close these past few days. I am just glad that Donald is a nice guy. This has been the happiest I've seen Keisha since the birth of Ned.

Time waits for no one. Before, we knew it, it was time to go to bed. So, we all hugged, said a night prayer, and wished each other a good night. I followed Keisha to her room. She shared the room with Cynthia and Ned. While Keisha got ready for bed we talked for a little while.

"I noticed lately that you and Donald have been chatting it up. Is there something you would like to share with your big cousin?" I leaned over to talk in her ear.

She then looked at me and with a slight grin on her face she remarked,

"I knew it would be just a matter of time before someone would be nosey enough to ask. Alright, yes, we like each other. Well, we enjoy talking to each other. We have exchanged numbers and agreed to keep in touch. Then over his summer break, he is coming to visit Ned and me. We will take our time and see what happens. Are you happy now?" Keisha turned her back and began placing the baby's things in a bag.

Just then Cynthia said with great excitement and in a baby's voice.

"I saw them kissing today when they thought we were all gone from out of the room."

She then started making kissing noises. I joined in with the teasing.

"All right, all right, enough," said Keisha as we laughed.

"Well, I better leave before we wake up the baby. Good night, ladies," I said while waving and walking out of the room.

That night I slept peacefully. I was sad that they were leaving today, but I have so many great memories to last me until we meet again. I was happy to know that Keisha found a good man. He might be a little younger than her but he is a good guy. He has a big heart, and he's a Christian with great plans.

The Curve

I woke up later that morning to someone screaming. It scared me so bad that my heart was beating so fast. I barely got out of bed when someone banged on my bedroom door.

"Get up Mom, hurry up, oh God! MOM! quick. Someone come here hurry up!" Cynthia was screaming. She was hysterical.

I opened the door and saw everyone running in all directions. I was screaming,

"What, what happened?" No one answered me. I did notice Cynthia crying with her hands on her face. Just then I heard Beverly telling Ricky to call 911. Then it seemed like time froze. I seem to be walking slower into Cynthia's bedroom. I heard screams and crying. What could have happened? We had such a wonderful visit. I tried to survey the scene. Everyone was running in all directions. That is when I noticed Keisha on the floor holding baby Ned. I flew to where she was. I saw the baby in her arms. I did not see that Louise was administering CPR. I wanted to ask but could not get the words out. I did not know what was happening but I started crying too. Then I heard a loud knock on the door. Two EMTs came in. They laid the baby down and asked all of us to move back. Donald picked Keisha up off the floor. The cops were in the living room speaking with Albert. Then the EMTs passed me with the baby. Keisha went with them. The rest of us followed.

We all crammed ourselves into Ricky and Donald's trucks. I do not even remember getting dressed. I looked out the window. I heard Ricky,

Beverly, and Albert, with her. I could not imagine what she was going through. How must she feel? What was going through her mind?

We arrived at the hospital by the grace of God because both vehicles were speeding and flying through red lights. We got there a little after the ambulance and police car. Eloise being a nurse stepped into action. She was talking with one of the medical staff when the police asked her to speak with her. We were all sitting in the waiting room. I have never seen my family so quiet. Even the children were sitting patiently waiting for any news. What seemed like an eternity later Eloise came back. She looked so solemn. Albert stood up and wrapped his arms around his wife.

"Bae," he asked.

"What is going on?" Albert just held Eloise in his arms.

"Ned died from SIDS," Eloise said as she scanned the room with her eyes. She went on to say.

"He must have died late last night or early this morning. They will let us know. Right now we have to be there for Keisha she is inconsolable."

Eloise was just about to say something else when Keisha came into the room accompanied by a doctor.

"I am truly sorry for your loss. Can someone please drive her home? She is in no state to be driving or left alone." The doctor shook Keisha's hand and passed her a paper. Before he left Ricky asked a question.

"Excuse me, doc. What exactly is SIDS? How or where did a 3-month-old baby catch it from?" Ricky looked like if he said any more he would burst into tears.

The doctor looked at all of us and said,

"It is not something you catch. It is called sudden infant death syndrome. It means exactly that. A baby under the age of 1 can suffocate and die at any unknown time. I gave Ms. Maddon some brochures explaining what it is. It is an obstruction to the airway. It happens to healthy and sick babies. It is undetected and has no warning signs." The doctor was in mid-sentence when there was a knock at the door.

The officer who took down all of our statements entered into the room.

"Well, we have all that we need. You all are free to go. Once again I am sorry for your loss," The officer shook our hands and with the doctor, they left the room.

Ricky helped Keisha up to her feet. I grabbed all the paperwork that was presented to her. I just felt so empty. I could only imagine what she must have been going through.

The car ride home was so silent. What should have been a more cheerful day turned out to be a mess. Finally, the silence was broken with the sobbing from Keisha. It was understandable that she was brokenhearted. I held her in my arms. She placed her head on my shoulders. Oh, she smelled like baby lotion. Then tears started to drop down my face. I did not know what to say to her. I just sat there stroking her hair and crying quietly to myself.

There was so much to think about. Eloise pulled some strings and made plans for the mortuary to come and retrieve the baby's body. I contacted my job and requested a couple of days off. I wanted to help them and Keisha. I could not believe that beautiful baby was now gone. I am happy that I spent so much time with him.

The days went by quickly. The funeral was very nice. The storm clean-up is coming along. It will be some time before everything, and everyone is back to some type of normalcy. I have seen a change in Keisha. I was trying to convince her to get some therapy. She just keeps claiming that she is alright.

As for me, things went back to normal quickly. I was once alone again. Cynthia found herself an after-school job. She got involved in extracurricular activities, and she also has a boyfriend. Red comes home more often now to check up on me. He told me that Donald and Keisha were getting closer. I am happy for her. Having him in her life will not take the place of her baby but it will help her not to feel alone.

About three months went by and I haven't heard from Keisha. I tried calling and leaving messages, and I sent texts. So, I informed Red so he could check on her for me. Cynthia and I had already planned a trip to visit them next month. I couldn't wait that long to hear something. Red finally called me with some news. Keisha said she has been busy. She will call you soon because she wants to visit. That made me so very happy.

Finally, about a week later Keisha did call me. She said she had some important news she wanted to tell me. I begged her to tell me over the phone but she insisted that she wanted to do it in person. She also would have Donald with her. I found that to be interesting. I told Cynthia. She guessed just as I did that Keisha and Donald were getting married. I did not ask how long she would be visiting. I just knew that the day she was coming would be the day after Cynthia left. Cynthia was going with the church on a college tour of some local colleges in the state. She would be gone for the weekend.

The days went by very quickly and I was helping Cynthia get ready. I would usually be saddened at the ideal of her leaving but I wasn't because tomorrow Keisha and Donald were coming. This time I would have Keisha stay in Red's old room so she would not have to deal with the memory of her son dying in Cynthia's room.

The next day I was so excited to see Keisha again I barely could sleep. I was up early. Every time I heard a car drive by I ran to the window. Then finally they arrived. I ran outside and gave her a big hug and kissed her on the cheek. I hugged Donald also. We went inside the house. I asked Keisha if she was comfortable with staying at the house. If not I could get her a hotel room for the weekend. Once she convinced me she was okay I directed her to Red's bedroom. Donald would be staying in the guest room.

Friday flew by so quickly. Saturday came and I had so many plans for us. I was trying to keep us from being in the house too long. We went to the Flea Market and a boat tour ride of the historic parts of the town. Keisha said she was tired and wanted to go back home to rest. I dropped them off back home and I went to pick up something for dinner. I wanted to surprise her with food from her favorite restaurant.

When I got back to the house it was dark. I opened the door and called for Donald and then for Keisha. That was strange, no one answered. Their car was still in the driveway. Then I turned on the lights as I went down the hall. I called for Keisha again. She finally answered.

"I blew a fuse and Donald is trying to find the fuse box," Keisha explained as she peeped outside her room door.

"Oh, you guys scared me. The fuse box is in here by the laundry door. I will fix it." I said, as I turned to walk back, I was hit across the back of my head.

I woke up with my hands tied behind my back and with a cloth in my mouth. I was so confused because my head was hurting and Keisha did it. I looked up and there she was standing over me. I so wanted to say something but my mouth was gagged. Keisha bent over and took the cloth out. I mustered up the strength to ask what was going on.

"You want to know what is going on!" Keisha said as she bent down to get in my face. "I'll tell you what is going on, You KILLER!" Keisha started to tell me an amazingly crazy story.

Once she got back home from the funeral for her son she had too much time to think. She thought about how I put her son to bed that night. It was me who spent most of the time with him. I was with him and did almost everything for him while they stayed with me. The more she thought the more her mind played a cruel joke. She started to imagine me being jealous of her. I was envious of her dating Donald and also having a baby when I could no longer have one. Then she convinced Donald that I wanted to harm her by harming her baby. She explained to me that she came up with this scheme. She also asked Donald to come along to see that everything went as planned.

She found out from Cynthia that she would be gone this weekend. Then Donald told her that Red would not be here either. So, this weekend would be the perfect weekend to do away with me.

I just sat there in shock. I could not believe what I was hearing. Keisha thought I could harm her in such a way that I would kill her son. I went to close my eyes for a second. It was hard to process what was going on. Just as I closed my eyes Keisha slapped me.

"Open your eyes and pay attention! I want you to hear everything that I have to say. I loved you like a mother, no like a sister, no like a best friend and you would do this to me." Keisha was so mad that her face looked distorted.

"Keisha, listen to me, please listen to me! I would never hurt you or that beautiful baby. I love you so much. I couldn't believe that you would think this of me. Let's go to therapy together. You are just grieving. Your mind is playing tricks on your reality." I was trying to talk fast because I could see that she did not care.

Just then Keisha looked me dead in my eyes and said the most unthinkable thing.

"I am going to kill you and then I am going to kill your baby like you killed mine. Do you understand me?" Keisha said as she grabbed my shirt by the neck.

Donald gripped her arm. He looked confused.

"Wait, you said nothing about killing anyone. You said that you just wanted to scare her so she could think about what she had done to you. If we kill anyone we will surely go to jail. Let's stick to our plans and leave." Donald was trying his best to persuade her to abandon this new plot.

"You are so weak. I thought you were stronger than this." Keisha pushed away from him. It doesn't matter. I will never stop until she hurts like I do.

"Are you serious?" I said. "I hurt every day. Every time I pass that room I hurt. I have talked to you almost every day since the accident. You said nothing about how deep your pain was. We could be helping each other heal." I started crying at this point because I was scared and because I couldn't believe that she had not once told me that her feelings were this bad.

Then I looked at Donald but before I could say anything to him, she put the rag back in my mouth. She grabbed me by the arm and gestured me to get up. We walked past the kitchen to the back door. She unlocked the door and pushed me outside. She told me to walk towards the back fence. We got beside the big oak tree. She told Donald to watch me. Then she went into the house.

I looked at Donald and tried to persuade him to help me with my eyes. He then began speaking to me.

"Look, I am so sorry. It was not supposed to go this way. We were just supposed to scare you so that you would feel deeply sorry for the part you played in her son's death. I will try to get her back to the original plan of just scaring you but play cool. Here she comes," he quickly said as he acted as if he was roughing me up some.

At this point, I was just numb. I so wish I could call someone anyone at this moment. Then all of a sudden as if time was going slow things started to happen. I heard Red calling me. I tried to sit up nice and tall so he could see me in the backyard, but I was too short. Then Keisha busted out of the back door and ran towards Donald and me. I could see that she had something in her hands and she was screaming.

"No, I am going to kill her. I am going to kill her!" Keisha screamed as she ran towards me.

"Stop this is the police!" a police officer said. He was coming from around the house screaming back at Keisha. "Put the weapon down!"

Just then I noticed that she had a gun in her hand. She went to raise it and she fell to the ground. I heard the gun went off. I closed my eyes because I thought for sure the bullet was coming for me. I did not feel anything. I opened my eyes to find Red was standing over me. Donald had his hands up in the air. The cops surrounded Keisha.

Then I heard someone say get the paramedics. Who was already in pursuit coming from the driveway? I tried to look, but could not see. Then I saw a glimpse of Keisha. She was lying on the ground. I saw her body twitched for a second and then stopped. What was I seeing? Did she get shot or just hurt from falling?

Red finally took the rag from around my mouth. I wanted to speak but couldn't. I just gasped for air. Then a wave of tears filled my eyes. I put my head into Red's chest. I couldn't stop crying. I was almost hysterical with emotions. The paramedics wanted me to get checked out at the hospital. I just wanted to see Keisha. I asked if I could see her one more time. I walked over to where she lay. You know when you see someone get shot on TV it looks bad, but I was not prepared for what I saw. The bullet went through her eye and came out through the back of her head. Blood, guts, and skin I don't know what it was but it was everywhere. There she lay on the stretcher. I felt sick. Just then I threw up and fainted because I woke up in the hospital.

I woke up to see Cynthia lying with her hands around me. Red was sitting on the sofa next to the window.

"Hey babies," I said smiling at the both of them.

"Mom, I am so glad that you are ok." Said Cynthia.

Red got up, came over, and stood by the bed.

"Hey, mom. You were so tired. You slept the rest of the day. Are you hungry?" he said while smiling gently towards me.

I sat up and squinted my eyes to adjust to the light in the room.

"Yes, I am hungry and thirsty." I wanted to ask about Keisha but was scared to bring it up. So, I pretended as if nothing happened. Just then a nurse came in.

"Good morning, Ms. Reynolds. You had a nasty experience yesterday. However, we have to get you better so that your children can bring you home in a couple of days. Let me check your vitals, then we will get you something to eat and drink. We have an IV in you right now but as soon as it is finished, we will take it out. How are you feeling? Are you experiencing any pain anywhere?" the nurse asked.

I just shook my head. I did not want to talk about it, and I know that is where she was trying to lead me. I wanted to forget all about it.

Just then Cynthia showed me a menu and asked, "Mom what do you want to eat?"

The nurse left after saying that someone would come to get my food order and that a doctor would come to talk to me soon. Once the nurse left we filled out the food order and then Red said to me as he pulled a chair up to get close to the bed.

"Mom, I am so sorry that this happened to you. Unfortunately, it is just the beginning. The police want to speak with you about what happened. Then there will be the case against Donald. I also took it upon myself to get a psychiatrist to speak with you. I know that you always fought against depression. I don't want this to push you further into despair. We need you here, healthy, and strong." Red said as tears dripped down his face.

I realized that it was not going to be a smooth ride. I finally found the strength to talk with Red and Cynthia about what happened. I was home now secured in my bedroom. I called them into my room and began recalling the events from the day. But, then Red said something that startled me. I was discussing with them what Donald said, "This is not how it was supposed to be," when Red interrupted.

"Mom, Donald told me that Keisha wanted to cause bodily harm to you. That she blamed you for little Ned's death. Donald told me a couple of days before it was going to happen. I set it up for him to go along with it so we could catch her in the act." Before Red could finish Cynthia jumped in.

"Wait a minute. You knew that Keisha and Donald were going to try to harm mom? Why, didn't you try to stop it beforehand?" I can't believe this shit! You allowed Mom to go through this pain, hell, Keisha died and it could have all been avoided. I just can't." Cynthia at this point was screaming, crying, and pacing the floor.

I had to intervene. I went over to Cynthia and just hugged her. I looked at Red and asked if he had finished what he was saying. Cynthia pulled away from me. Before she could say another word, I put my finger to my mouth. This suggested to her to be quiet.

He called me the day before Keisha and Donald were to come. He told me everything. It started the day that Ned died. She told Donald that you must have done something to him. She did not believe the doctor's theory that a healthy child could die in their sleep. He was fine until you laid him down that night. She also said that it was the only day that you took care of him all day. Even at the funeral, she said you did not look so upset. That is when she came up with the idea of making you feel her pain." Red paused and walked over to the window.

I just sat there in total amazement that my cousin would think such a thing. I also tried to speak with her because I knew that she suffered from depression like I did. She never said anything. I did not want to hear any more but my human curiosity needed to be fed. Just then Red turned around and continued with his story.

"Donald told me that she had changed. The new her scared him and he reached out to me because he believed that it was the right thing to do. He was at first following along with her for love. Then his morals stepped up and he realized that it was wrong. He hoped, that once she saw you and heard your side of the story, she would stop the madness. It did not work out that way." Red was now sitting on the bed next to me. He took my right hand and was holding it.

I was listening to every word. Something just wasn't settling with me. Red decided to wait. If he knew she felt this way he should have told someone. We could have met with her as a family and got it out in the open. I just can't believe this happened to me. Then I was mad with Red, but he was here and I was determined to ask him why he didn't say anything.

"So, let me see if I understood. Donald told you of the plans a couple of days before the event. Why did you not tell me? We could have saved my cousin and she might still be alive today." Tears started to drip down my face. All I could do was shake my head. I was very upset.

"That is what I am wondering too, " said Cynthia.

"I do not know. I thought I was doing something. I felt like if we caught her in the act, maybe we could convince her to see that this action was wrong. I left school and when I got closer to the house my spirit led me to call the police and inform them of what was happening. I did not expect it to end this way. I did not think this though. I am truly sorry. I will never forget this for the rest of my life. NEVER!" Red just broke down and cried. At this point, we were all crying.

I hated to go on but I needed to. Especially, while we were already talking about it.

"What do you think should be done about Donald? I asked Red. I know that he was part of the problem but then he tried to reconcile it.

"Well, he knows that he will face charges. I'm hoping that you could ask for leniency towards his punishment. He is a good guy. He just made a bad choice. I want the judge to go easy on him. He just got caught up with being loved by someone like Keisha." Red then shrugged his shoulders.

I did not ask Cynthia because I already knew her answer. She would say throw the book at him. I just needed time to pray about it. The conversation ended there and was not picked up again until before Donald's trial. It would be nice to say that everything and everybody returned to normal afterward, but that would be a lie.

It has been 5 years and the whole family has never gotten over Keisha. Red, by the way still, speaks with Donald. Donald received 10 years for his involvement in the plot. He does have a chance for early parole. Red graduated from college last year. He is now focusing on opening up a restaurant. Cynthia who is now a junior in college is doing well. She has blossomed into a beautiful young woman. Ricky, Beverly, and the children are doing much better now. It was rough after the storm. Their business and home were destroyed and he had to start all over. The insurance was reluctant to pay the full value price. So, Ricky sued and won a big settlement. Albert and Eloise are doing just fine. Albert started a little business with Eloise while he waited for Ricky's business to re-open. They are designers. Who would have guessed that Albert has good taste? Their business is doing so well that he is working part-time for Ricky. Eloise is doing the design business full-time because she is making more money. Plus, they are adding a new addition to the Maddon Clan this Spring, wait for it, TWINS! We are all excited. I decided not to get too attached to their children. It is a whole story I am going through with my therapist. Keisha's parents Dixie and George are not doing so well. Dixie had a major breakdown after Keisha and Ned's death. The whole ordeal about Ned dying, Keisha plotting to kill me, and then accidentally shooting herself was just too much for her. George is trying to remain calm through it all. However, he does not seem well. His health is deteriorating. He suffers from bad dreams and insomnia, and he can't eat. As a family, we visit them at least once a month. I call them every week. It is not easy to lose a loved one to death, but to lose your only child and grandchild all in a short amount of time. It is putting a strain on their marriage.

Then there is me. How is Trisha Reynolds doing? She is not well. I lost my favorite cousin, I was blamed for the death of her son, and my son as far as my mind goes, I feel that he played a part in it or at least he could have made better choices. First, I have never been the same since the baby died. I keep re-living all the events that led up to my last hug with him. Oh, what a gift from God he was. Such a happy baby. He barely ever cried. I secretly blamed myself. Even though there was no evidence of foul play. Somehow I just blamed myself. Maybe it was because I was the last person to have physical contact with him. I do not know. I know that I felt guilty.

Then whenever I spoke with Keisha over the phone, I knew something was not right but I thought it was over losing a child. I would never have dreamt that it was over me. Then when Keisha came to my house to visit me something did not feel right. I just could not put my finger on the problem. My beautifully, smart, funny, sweet cousin who I used to carry around my hip hated me. OH, every time I think about that fatal day when she accidentally shot herself. How she died thinking I killed her son. I realized that our relationship went from love to hate. It just tears me up inside. I only pray that God forgives both of our actions.

Then there is the issue of my son's part in knowing that someone wanted to do his mom harm and he allowed it to take place. I don't know, maybe I am wrong. I know he thinks that he did the right thing. He wanted to catch Keisha in the act. He wanted her to see the wrong in her actions. He wanted me to see how Keisha was now. This incident could have been avoided if he had come home a day earlier or called to warn me. Well, it is over and done. I do not understand what the concept was in waiting. I know I must spend the rest of my life wondering what if. My therapist suggested to me a support group for women who have faced any tragedy in their lives.

The support group is nice. I have been attending for about 3 months. I have met some incredible women. Through their friendship, I have made so many friends. These women call me, we go out together, and we volunteer at a women's shelter. I am finally starting to live the life I always wanted. I still have bouts of depression, but it does not last long. So the question was how is Trisha Reynolds doing? She is not well but she will be. Oh, I also left out something important. At the shelter, I also help women work through their depression. It is not so much a therapy group but a group where we talk and let go of any baggage that will hold us back. This is something that I wished Keisha and I would have done after Ned's death. However, none of us thought about it. Everyone everywhere will face some form of depression. Depending on how you manage your depression. Determines if it makes or breaks you.

This incident is something that I will never forget. I think it will make a good book. I want people to feel the tragedy of both women. I want people to learn to communicate their feelings and not let them fester. However, the most tragic in this story were the men. Donald and Red both had opportunities to come forth and stop the incident before so many lives were damaged. I want to go on to write other books, but I hope the subject matter is never this intense and personal again.

Maybe I will be a good author. I know that I do not have much time for daydreaming.

About the Author

Author Celeste Ross is a single mother of 2. Her inspiration to push forward is her children, Sheree and Malik. She is an ex-educator with over 10 years of experience. She had always looked for ways to encourage her children and her students. A student at Liberty University. She is a member of Omega Nu Lambda, an online honor society, LU's School of Education, and LU's Alumni Community. She is also an active member of Shekinah Tabernacle Church, Inc. where she is the current head of the Outreach Team. Check out her YouTube channel: https://www.youtube.com/@Celebratingmylife10 28

Email grcero03@gmail.com

Trisha Reynolds is starting to realize the notion that she will soon be an Empty Nester. Her last child Cynthia will be in college soon. Trisha already feels lonely and depressed most of the time. The thought of both of her children being gone is just too much to bear. Life will deal Trisha a happy blow. A tropical storm will send her beloved relatives to stay with her. Trisha is particularly excited about her favorite cousin Keisha arriving with her 3-month-old baby boy. Unfortunately, the weather isn't the only storm that is brewing. So much tragedy will erupt within this small family. Some will lose property and employment, and lives will be forever changed. Someone will make a poor judgment call that will end a life. Trisha will find heartbreak. She will have to redirect her life to save her sanity. How will she be able to trust again? Her faith will be tested. Her cousin Keisha will find love but is it real? Keisha will deal with her private demons as she makes life choices. The other family members will wrestle with their problems. No one will be able to see the troubles that lie ahead.

www.ingramcontent.com/pod-product-compliance
Lightning Source LLC
Chambersburg PA
CBHW061735250726

48657CB00002B/933